Dumble The Dinosaur
or, How Chocolate Was First

by Sue Heaser
Music and Editing by Alison Hedger

A musical play with six songs for young children involving mime, dance and percussion.

Duration approx. 25 mins.
For children aged 4 - 8 years.
Key Stages 1 + Lower 2

TEACHER'S BOOK
Music and production notes.
Ideas for appraisal of the music are included.

SONGS

1. Dumble The Dinosaur *Drums and chimes*
2. We Are Cavemen *Woodblock*
3. Round And Round *Dance plus pitched percussion*
4. Terry The Dactyl *Recorder counter melody*
5. Rattle, Rattle *Maracas, guiro and drum*
6. Chock-Rock *Hand jiving*

Considerable licence has been taken with the chronology, facts and the portrayed discovery of chocolate in this light-hearted story involving dinosaurs and ancient man. .

"I hope Dumble The Dinosaur will bring your pupils much fun. My own pupils, for whom the musical was written, enjoyed every moment - from the preparing of the songs and costumes to the performances for their families and friends. The fact that chocolate is an irresistible food to many people, may have something to do with the musical's attraction - who knows?" Sue Heaser

The Pupil's Book, Order No. GA10678, contains the narrative, dramatised scenes and song words.

A matching tape cassette of the music for rehearsals and performances is also available, Order No. GA10694, side A with vocals included and side B with vocals omitted.

© Copyright 1993 Golden Apple Productions
A division of Chester Music Limited
8/9 Frith Street, London W1V 5TZ

Order No. GA10621
ISBN 0-7119-3388-X

DUMBLE THE DINOSAUR

CAST LIST

Non-speaking:

Cavemen
Cave-women
Cave-children
Dumble the Dinosaur (3 children)
Baby Dinosaur

Speaking:

Terry the Dactyl
Chip the Caveboy (or girl)
Mrs. Cobble (Chip's Mother)

Stoney
Flinty } Cave-people
Rocky

Sandie
Pebble } Cave-children
Boulder

PROPS LIST

Spears and clubs for Cavemen
Pots and sticks for Cave-women
Large bowl and stick for Chip
Leaves, stalks and "milk" to make Chock-Rock
Pieces of chock-rock
Large yellow dinosaur egg

APPRAISAL OF MUSIC

"I have included a few ideas on how to use the music constructively to develop appraisal. Ask the children whether they like the songs or not, giving reasons for their views. No answer will be right or wrong — we are all entitled to an opinion. Ask whether the music and lyrics reflect the moods and characters, and set the children listening out for melody shapes and speeds. Are there any points in the piano part which may have been a little unexpected? Take a hand count on the favourite song. Also take the opportunity of groups of children criticising their own singing and playing. A tape recorder will come in useful. Never offend or embarrass a child who cannot manage a certain skill — with careful handling the critique session can be full of laughs but also revealing to the children themselves. I hope this little musical will provide schools with a valuable educational resource which is also a happy and memorable production for teachers, children and audiences."

Alison Hedger 1993

PRODUCTION NOTES

INTRODUCTION

The musical is a lighthearted fantastical entertainment and in no way an historical or authentic representation of how things were in the distant past. The authors are aware of the chronological inaccuracies! Please see the notes at the back of the book on the history of dinosaurs, flying reptiles, cavemen and chocolate.

THE SONGS

All the children join in with every song, whether on stage or not. The words are deliberately repetitive for the youngest of performers to cope with easily. Most of the songs have actions — suggestions for these are given in the script, but the children might like to develop their own ideas.

THE PIANO PART

This has been kept as simple as possible whilst remaining a pleasant accompaniment. Please feel free to embellish and build upon it as desired. Guitar chords are also given.

PERCUSSION AND SOUND EFFECTS

Use the percussion instruments to give body and colour to the songs. Never let the percussion players drown the words. Some simple percussion parts are given and Song 4 has a countermelody for recorder which can be played by an older child or another member of staff. If you are using an electronic keyboard for special sound effects, the countermelody can be played on this with a suitable voice such as Trumpet. A tape recorder can be used for playing pre-recorder noises for Dumble's loud roar and the cracking of the large egg.

PROPS

Involve the children in the making of their spears, clubs, bowls etc. Use papier-mâché for Dumble's egg and for chunks of chock-rock. Chip can mime most of the giving out of chock-rock.

SCENERY

Only one set is needed with a cave entrance to the rear. Suggest the jungle by decorating one side of the acting area with large leafy branches. These can be created out of paper, or use real branches standing in buckets filled with large stones.

COSTUMES

All the costumes can be made economically by using old curtains, bedspreads, sheets and pillowcases. The cave-people wear a simple tunic belted at the waist with garden twine. Pillowcases with head and arm holes are ideal. Some tunics can be cut to cover only one shoulder. Use earthy colours like dark greens, browns and ochres to decorate the tunics. The children will enjoy painting their own costume to look muddy, grubby and frayed! Alternatively paint large spots and stripes to represent animal skins. For the cavemen either make large cotton wool beards painted all types of hair colour, (don't forget red beards!) or use face paints to give stubbly chin growth. You might even like to highlight eyebrows. Use hair gel and hair spray to create suitably wild and spiked hairstyles. The cave-women can have paper flowers in their hair and wear necklaces made by themselves of threaded leaves, sticks, feathers and flowers. The cavemen might like to wear necklaces of large white teeth!

Mrs. Cobble can wear an apron to differentiate her from the other cave-women. Chip may like to think of a way in which he/she can be different to other children, by adding a special touch to his/her costume. Special anklets or wrist bands perhaps?

All cave-people have bare legs and feet.

TERRY THE DACTYL

The colours of Pterodactyls are unknown, so make Terry as bright and as colourful as you like. Attach fabric wings to the elbows and little fingers by elastic. An enormous beak is essential.

DUMBLE THE DINOSAUR

Use three or more children. The costume is created much like a Chinese Dragon. The children hold the waist of the one in front and are covered by one large piece of material, which looks effective if covered by paper or fabric scales. The covering is best at knee length so that colourful tights add interest to the costume. The body children also need to be able to extend a hand to receive a piece of chock-rock, and one of the children must be able to carry and pass out the large dinosaur egg.
Dumble's head is worn by the first child and is best created out of a large cardboard box. Painted ping-pong balls make good eyes. A large tail for thumping in the appropriate places by the end child, hangs down behind. A sand-filled tail will give a good thump.

DUMBLE'S BABY

Choose the smallest child. Green sweater and tights look good, with a face mask made from a cardboard box.

You may prefer all the children wearing tights to have the feet removed for safety.

THE SET

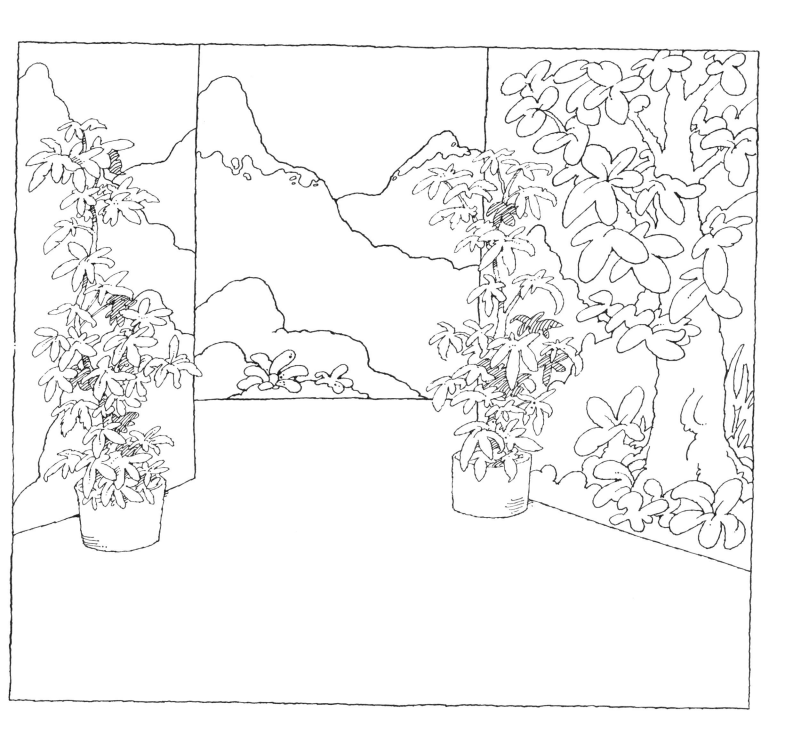

SONG 1   DUMBLE THE DINOSAUR

Cue: *Stage remains empty for the first song*

Chimes F♯ and G for CHORUS only

Drums:

Cue: FINALE *for exits and bow takes place after word of thanks to cast.*

Happily ♩ = 80

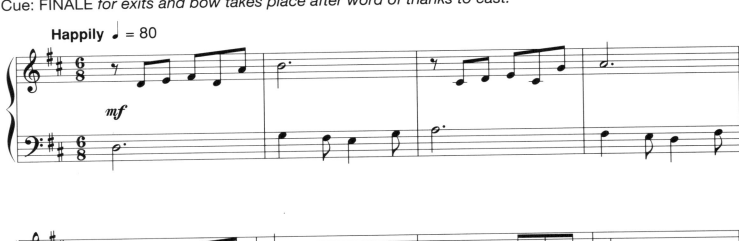

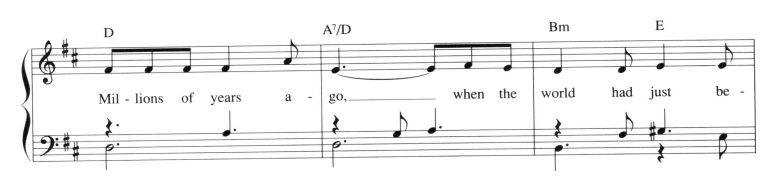

Mil - lions of years a - go,_____ when the world had just be -

- gun,   There lived a di - no - saur, Dum - ble the di - no - saur,

Listen carefully to the music which is played after the song and compare it with the music which is played before the song. Are they the same?

WE ARE CAVEMEN

Cue: *Cave-women and cave-children take up stage positions chanting*
"Where are the cavemen?"

With strength ♩ = 104

1. We are cave - men march - ing in the sun.
2. We are cave - men walk - ing in the sun.

We are cave - men march - ing in the sun. We are cave - men
We are cave - men walk - ing in the sun. We are cave - men

march - ing in the sun, We car - ry our spears. We fear no one!
walk - ing in the sun, We brand - ish our clubs. We fear no one!

To finish

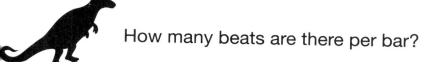

How many beats are there per bar?

Does having 4 beats per bar make the music good to march and walk to?

Which words are used to rhyme with sun? (Ans: one, everyone, done, fun.)

Think of more words to rhyme with sun. (Bun, gun, won, ton, stun . . .)

Caveman   Cave-woman   Cave-child

3.   We are cave-women sitting in the sun . . .
       Preparing the food for everyone.

4.   We are cave-children playing in the sun . . .
       We play away, 'til the day is done.

5.   We are cave-people dancing in the sun . . .
       We bob up and down. We have great fun!

The woodblock follows the rhythmic pattern of the words

ROUND AND ROUND

Cue: "... *and then played games in the afternoon.*"

3. Skip and choose a partner

4. We all clap and have fun

5. La la la la, la la

Two optional parts for pitched percussion

Notes used:

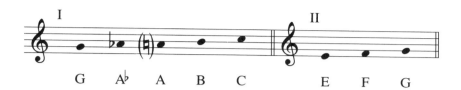

G   A♭   A   B   C   E   F   G

Verse one should be sung without the counter-melodies. Bring in the other 2 melodies as desired, but never drown the main theme.

Alternatively the tunes could be sung or hummed by a small group. This may happen spontaneously by those playing the counter-melodies on chime bars, glockenspiels or metallophones. You will then have achieved singing in 2 or 3 parts!

TERRY THE DACTYL

Cue: *Suddenly Terry the Dactyl appeared in the sky and swooped all around.*

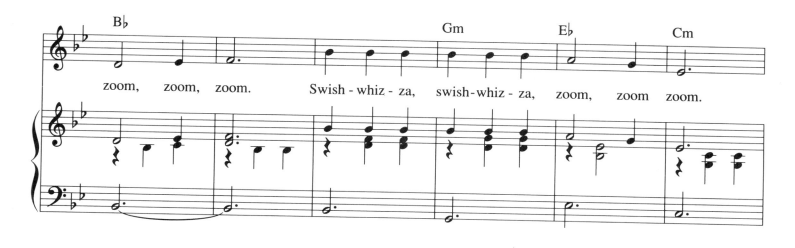

zoom,   zoom,   zoom.   Swish - whiz - za, swish-whiz - za, zoom,   zoom   zoom.

First time   **To finish**

Whiz   whiz   whiz.   whiz.

How many beats per bar for this song?
Does 3 beats per bar give a lilt to the music?
Is one of the 3 beats stronger than the others?

If so, which one? (Ans: the first $\frac{3}{4}$ ♩ ♩ ♩)
                                      1 2 3

Why is 3 time good for this song?
Does the music make you want to act out being Terry?

Recorder melody for CHORUS only

13

RATTLE, RATTLE

SONG 5

Cue: ". . . *dreadful news and wondered what they should do. Then suddenly. . .*"

From * to end is EXIT music for cave-people. (Script p.7)

Add maracas, guiro, shakers etc. to CHORUS only.
Drums or clapping at ⨯ . Stamping on the "thumps", with high knees, is fun.

2. The dinosaur seemed frightfully fierce,
    It gave an awful growl.
    The dinosaur seemed frightfully fierce,
    It made the children howl.

    IT WENT . . . (*Chorus*)

3. The dinosaur jumped up and then down,
    It chased them one by one.
    The dinosaur jumped up and then down,
    It made the women run.

    IT WENT . . . (*Chorus*)

How does the introduction depict a dinosaur?
Why is the dotted rhythm used in the Chorus effective?
Would plain quavers be just as good?

CHOCK-ROCK

Cue: *"I think I'll call it, chock-rock"*
Cue:*". . . became known as CHOCOLATE. The name remains to this very day!"*

Point out to the children that the left hand accompaniment for the introduction and CHORUS, has an ostinato (recurring pattern of notes) except for the last bar. See if they can count how many times the pattern is repeated.

(Ans: 9)

We'd like to eat it for our sup - per.___ We'd like to eat it for our

tea. We'd like to eat it in the morn - ing.___ We'd

eat and eat and eat it, you'd see.___

Return to Chorus

2. We'll nev - er need a lol - li - pop. We'll nev - er need an ice.

We'll just need our chock - y - rock, Be - cause it is so nice.

Chip skips around Dumble who bobs up and down to the music.

Chip

Dumble the Dinosaur

Enter Dumble . . . They then dance together
whilst everyone sings the Chorus from
Song 5   RATTLE, RATTLE

Baby Dinosaur

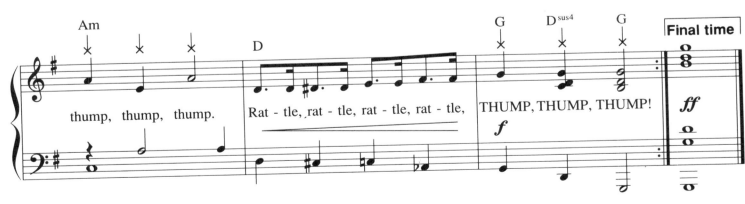

For the repeat of Song 6, CHOCK-ROCK, we need page 8 of the script, and pages 16-18 of this book. Please turn back.

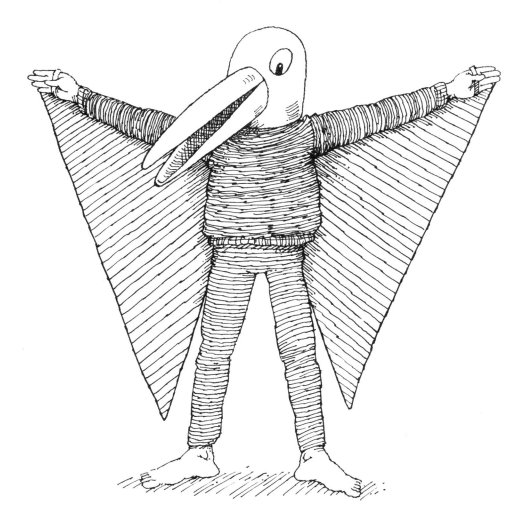

Terry the Dactyl

For the **FINALE** and taking of bows and exits, you will need to play
Song 1 DUMBLE THE DINOSAUR, pages 6 and 7 of this book.
Play as many times as required.

FACTS ABOUT PREHISTORIC MAN

1. Man and dinosaurs did not co-exist. Man is a relative new-comer on earth. His early ancestors first began making stone tools and building rough shelters in caves about 2.5 million years ago.

2. Neanderthal people, an early form of homo sapiens, first appeared about 125,000 years ago. They looked much like people today, wore clothes of animal skins, made flint tools and buried their dead. They are what most people think of as "cave men".

3. Neanderthals hunted wild animals for food and gathered plants and berries. They knew how to make fire and cook their food. They also would probably have used clubs of wood or bone for weapons.

4. Neanderthals lived in small groups in caves or in shelters made from branches or stones.

FACTS ABOUT DINOSAURS

1. Dinosaurs inhabited the earth between about 224 and 64 million years ago.

2. All our knowledge about dinosaurs is through their fossilised remains; some of their bodies became covered in mud after death and geological processes eventual converted the bones to fossils. We can date the fossils from the age of the rocks in which they are found.

3.   There were many different types of dinosaur and they varied greatly in size and shape. Their fossils have been discovered all over the world.

4.   Dinosaurs were reptiles; they had scaly skin and laid eggs. They lived on land and did not habitually swim, nor did they fly. (Flying reptiles or pterosaurs were not dinosaurs.)

5.   The last dinosaurs disappeared about 64 million years ago, 61.5 million years before the appearance of Stone Age man. Their mass extinction is still a mystery although many theories have been suggested such as climatic change or the collision of a vast meteorite with the earth. Many other creatures became extinct at the same time.

Dumble the Dinosaur would probably have been a plant-eating dinosaur, (hence her liking for chocolate) such as a Diplodocus or an Apatosaurus (originally called Brontosaurus). These huge dinosaurs were up to 27 metres long and lived around 145–64 million years ago.

Terry the Dactyl would have been a flying reptile; a Pterodactyl or Pterosaur. These creatures lived around 150–70 million years ago and had wings of stretched membrane and huge beaks. The largest had wing spans of up to 11 metres.

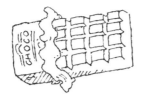 # FACTS ABOUT CHOCOLATE

1. Chocolate is made from the beans of the cacao tree which grows in South America. First, the beans are roasted, shelled and ground into a paste. Milk may be added for a milder flavour and the paste is then mixed with large quantities of sugar. Finally it is ground again for smoothness and the end result is chocolate.

2. The cacao tree was cultivated by the Indians of South America over 3000 years ago. They used the beans as money as well as making them into a bitter chocolate drink.

3. The Spaniards brought the drink to Europe in 1519 and in a sweetened form, it rapidly gained popularity all over Europe.

4. It was not until the 19th century that the processes for making eating chocolate, as we know it today, were developed.

9/07(634
Printed in Engla